Christmas is Coming!
Little Advent Coloring Book

Mary Lou Brown & Sandy Mahony

December 1

December 2

December 3

December 4

December 5

December 6

December 7

December 8

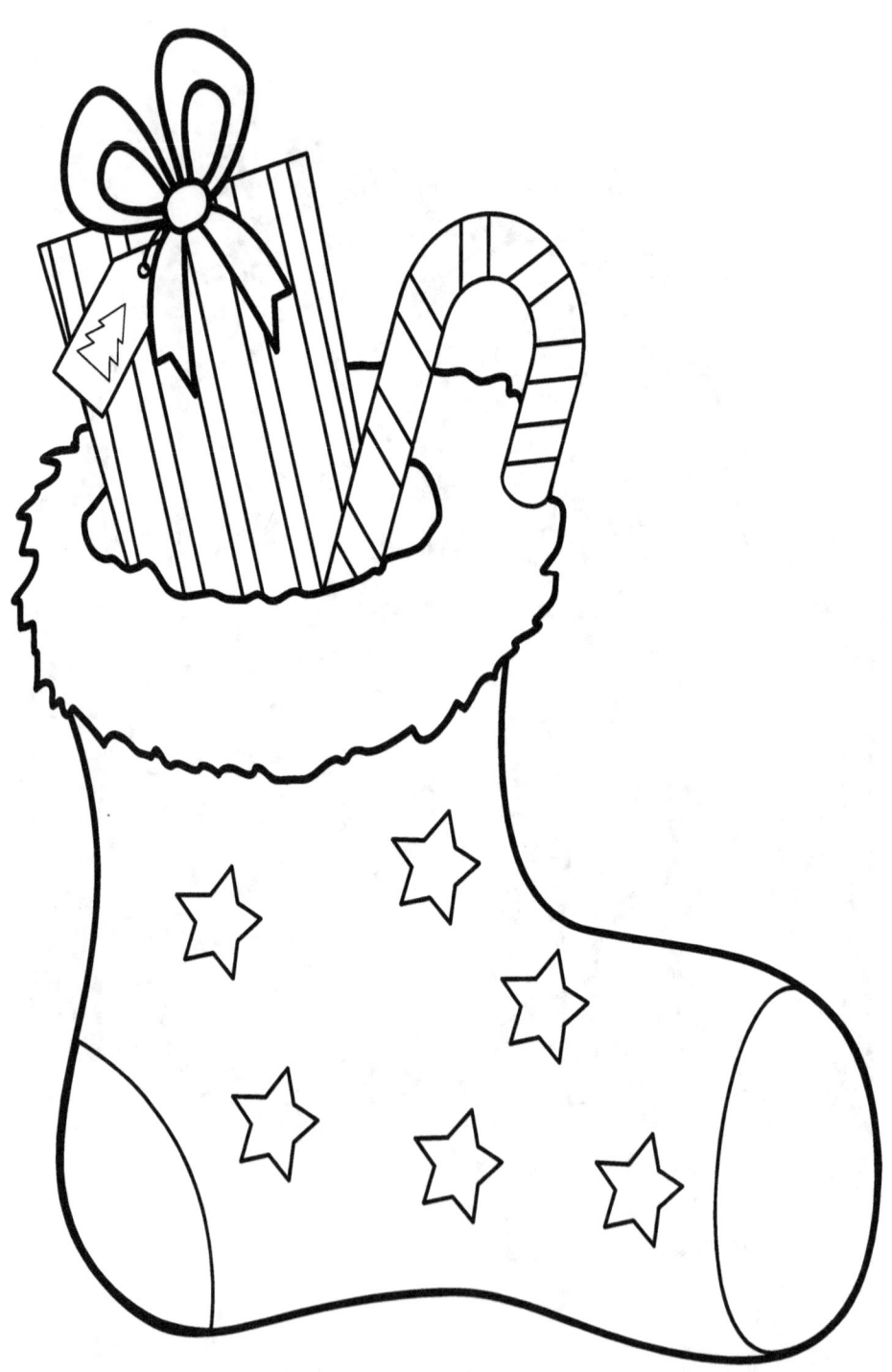

December 9

December 10

December 11

December 12

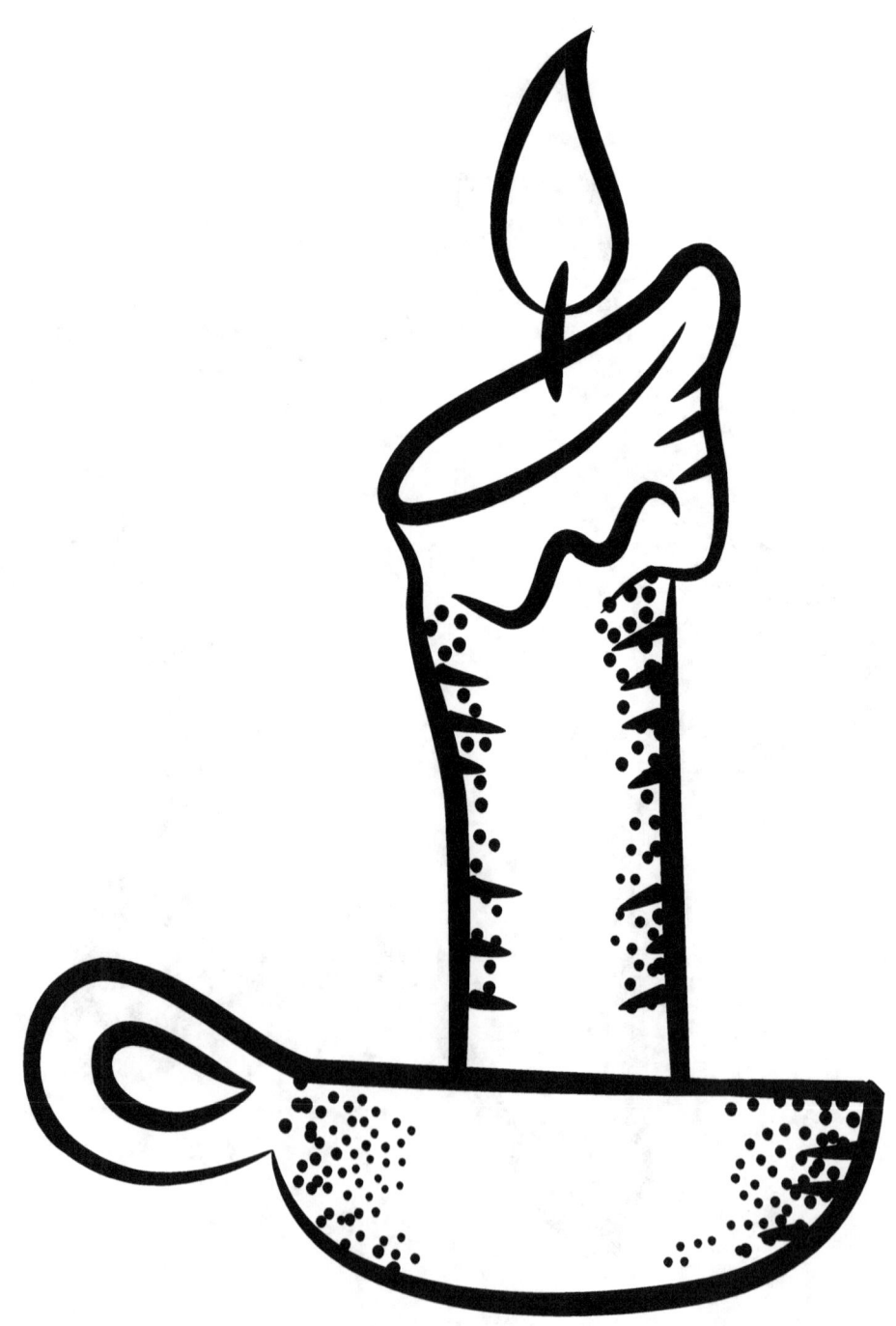

December 13

December 14

December 15

December 16

December 17

December 18

December 19

December 20

December 21

December 22

December 23

December 24

December 25

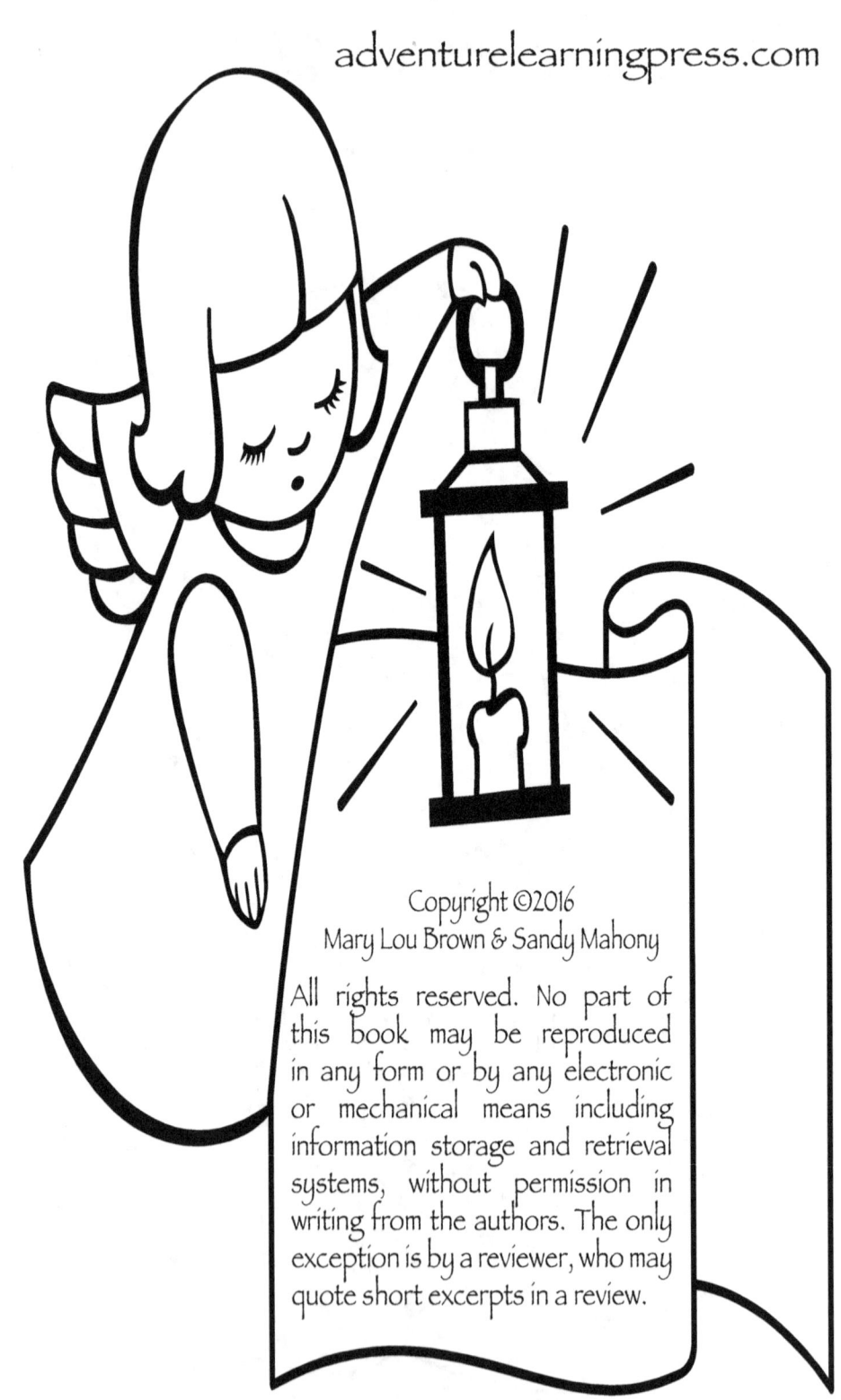

adventurelearningpress.com